Fred Owen
Visit to SA March 2002.

Keorapetse Kgositsile

IF I COULD SING
Selected Poems

Kwela / Snailpress

To all our mothers, daughters, wives, sisters,
'the rock-hard foundation of our struggle', as Madiba correctly says.
As long as any woman remains any patriarch's 'occupied territory'
A Luta Continua! Malibongwe!

And to the memory of
Baba Mabhida, Ntate Mashego, Tata O.R.,
Comrade Shope, and Chris Hani.
May your eye condemn us
till the end of time if we ever betray our mission.

Published by KWELA, P O Box 6525, Roggebaai, 8012, South Africa
in association with
SNAILPRESS, 30 Firfield Road, Plumstead, 7800, South Africa

© Keorapetse Kgositsile 2002
First edition, first printing 2002
ISBN 0-7957-0145-4

Poems selected by the author
Cover photograph by Annari van der Merwe
Cover design and typesetting by User Friendly
Set in 10 on 12 point Palatino
Printed and bound by Mills Litho, Maitland, Cape Town, 7405

CONTENTS

There are no sanctuaries except in purposeful action

FOREWORD

Keorapetse 'Willie' Kgositsile is a major poet whose life and poetic offerings are best contextualised within boundaries of a revolution: a movement for national liberation and majority rule in South Africa. This does not necessitate any special rubric to evaluate his work, however, since revolutions are rare and poets who participate in them as activists and artists are rarer still. Nevertheless a revolutionary poet deserves mentioning in the context of other revolutionary poets. When trying to find texts to compare Kgositsile with one thinks of Pablo Neruda of Chile, Garcia Lorca of Spain, Agostinho Neto of Angola, Okot P Bitek of Uganda and Thomas McGrath of the United States.

Kgositsile's work is complex: exploring a sense of impending impotence, anger, disgust, commitment, joy, love, metaphysical death, birth, confession, loss and an overriding need to participate concretely in struggles to liberate the land of his birth. These poems are no mere slogans. One might observe that their rhythms alone are both stunning and original; perhaps drawn from the insistence of an inner-ear sensitive to the possibility of utilising music and Setswana to affect poetic lines. These poetic texts are masterfully written evoking a superior orality and aurality. There is something magical about the way the personae of these poems seemingly start in one direction, reverse, or deviate to side paths, and then deftly start in an entirely different one to begin anew on another plane of reality. This is the work of a poet hearing his own muse and inventing an original expression as medium for the oracle. This is a distinguished, prolific, well-connected and internationally recognised poetic voice.

STERLING PLUMPP

ORIGINS

deep in your cheeks
your specific laughter owns
all things south of the ghosts
we once were. straight ahead

the memory beckons from the future
you and I a tribe of colours
this song   that dance
godlike rhythms to birth
footsteps of memory
the very soul aspires to. songs

of origins songs of constant beginnings
what is this thing called
love

SONG FOR MELBA

We grew then

And we said
Evil and then pain of evil
Be trampled underfoot
To ashes and dust ...

We grow

And the blood of the birth of laughter
Gives way to the face
Of the sons and daughters of our Sun
Till now in the stillnesses
– but not silence to the lover's eye –
Of our determined motion
Like the wind the face
Of our sons and daughters
Born every day like the sun
Moves on to their laughter
And the flow of their birth

And we grow

INDEED IN DEED

Across continents on fire
vampires fly against the wind
do we lack specific answer?

Oceans of memory
giantstep in upright path
the newborn infant asks which
way is the way to the way

The unrelenting tide sticky
as mountains of wax
giantsteps
to reclaim the childhood

We rebuild swallow-slow
but we rebuild
how deny specific deed is
specific answer? Speak!

OF DEATH AND LIVES

Some kind of hue
blue and thick as a minute
to the midnight   snakes death doses
across desire. Though some,
perhaps, do not know, this
voice rips apart the night

leaving silent evening bloodied
but every road leads some
place even at the darkest hour

Our passions now muddied haunt
the night with silent shrills only
the lover's eye can hear but
the finger of love moves on
relentless as the voice of lightning

There will be no hesitation
for communion at dawn, your nipples
salty with last night's stale
tears waving into my lips
searching for me in my breath

DEATH DOSES – 3

Days like this are
a system of hell
you need more
than a poem for a cure
treasures of recorded feeling
like that I have been through
agony is old
as the creation of feeling

I say days like this
are a system of hell
my heart cannot dance here
hear the very air stick its poison finger
in the inner regions of the heart
being, as I am, from every
where I have been, I say
later for similar possibilities

MY PEOPLE WHEN NOTHING MOVES

when nothing moves anywhere
the only motion is the noisy
stillness in me

should you then
          long for
              me
look for
    me

in forbidden songs
searching in the light
beyond petrified hypocrisies

OF US FOR US

I know my name
which denies no mask
made obsolete by ghouls
and oxford pants
that covered no balls
my name wore the mask
to hide the cowardly tear
and I know my name
celebrating all time love hate
measured in broken chains
leaping in your stride
lighting oceans of fire
in your face without veil
nor shadow between my name and the tide

WHEN BROWN IS BLACK

for Rap Brown

Are you not the light
that does not flicker
when murderers threaten summertime
passions of our time

Are you not the searchlight
in our eyes red with the dust
from the slave's empty grave
sending chills through
lynching johnsons around the world
as their obscene ghettos
go up in summertime flames

Some say it's youthful
adventure in the summertime
for they have lost natural instinct
which teaches a person to be free

What does a penny buy?

Are you not the fist
which articulates the passion
of the collective power of our rebirth
Are you not the fist
of the laughter of the rhythms
of the flames of our memory

What does a penny buy?

The naked head of the fuse
is up in the air pregnant
with the flaming children of our time
when Brown is Black
blowing up white myths
which built up layers of mists
which veiled the roads to the strength
of our laughter in the sun

But some
eating their balls in empty statements
say it is youthful
adventure in the summertime

Now we said
the game is over, didn't we?
when we reach the end of the line
the shit goes up in flames, don't I say?

What does a penny buy?

For Malcolm
for the brothers in Robben Island
for every drop of Black blood
from every white whip
from every white gun and bomb
for us and again for us
we shall burn
and beat the drum
resounding the bloodsong
from Sharpeville to Watts
and all points white of the memory
when the white game is over
and we dance to our bloodsong
without fear nor bales
of tinted cotton over our eye

Go on, brother, say it. Talk
the talk slaves are afraid to live

What does a penny buy?

When Brown is Black

BROTHER MALCOLM'S ECHO

Translated furies ring
on the page   not thoughts
about life
but what should be
real people and things
loving love
this is real
the human spirit moves
what should be
grinning molotov cocktails
replenishing the fire
Watts happening
Sharpeville burning

much too damn talking
is not
what's happening

MANDELA'S SERMON

Blessed are the dehumanised
for they have nothing to lose
but their patience

False gods killed the poet in me. Now
I dig graves
with artistic precision

TO FANON

Tears
hiding behind a doomed god
no longer define
the soul
because of your shock therapy
history's psychosis will be cured
once-soft shack-born melodies explode
in love-loving hollers
in the womb of the future
exposing the shallow trenches
of make-believe history to the fury
of the midday sun
and now lovers weaving
their dreams into infinite
realities with ghetto charms will
with the light of the poet
show jesus miracles

THE AIR I HEAR

The air, I hear,
froze to the sound
searching. And my memory
present and future tickles
the womb like the pulse
of this naked air
in the eye of a tear
drop. The dead cannot
remember even the memory
of death's laughter. But memory
defiant like the sound of pain
rides the wave at dawn
in the marrow of the desert
palm: stands looking still
and the bitter shape
of yesterdays weaves
timeless tomorrows
in the leaves
of laughter larger than
singular birth ...

SHOTGUN

Five deaths ago my
name was born
inside the thigh
of a breath. Over

300 years in the grip
of blood-drenched sweat I
walk the flesh of the future
like the heir's nimble
grin at diamond dust. And my
son playing in the nimble
leaves of the mimosa soil-bound

Over 300 years ... but every night
the red-lipped sun kisses the sea
the leaf mates even
with factory-filthed air   '
and love loves love
bathed in a drop of the sun
kissing the singing muscle
of the mine labourer's son

Over 300 years of deballed grins ...

Once-torture-twisted sighs
of uprooted orgasms
colour the air with riffs
of future pulse. Self-born
Maumau splits time's skull
with spearpoint flesh of mystic mask
of built-in shotgun weaved
in sounds like my daughter's
memory of anguished joy in nigger-
hard shadows screwing
the right moment ... Uptight
the raggedy-ass prophet says
everything is alright ...

MAYIBUYE IAFRIKA

like the memories
of fatherless black children
become fathers of desire
in fox-holes before
they are old enough to build
cattle by the riverbank

the dancing road
uncoils in the ear
pierced by the finger
of the slender smile
of tight roots ... these
retrieved eyes across the tight
belly of a pregnant drum
these are the words
of an ancient dancer of steel
the children of a person
share the head of a locust
and who cannot say
life is
an unfolding proverb
woven around
the desire of the memory
of the belly dance

I remember
the taste of desire
crushed like the dream
of ghetto orphans rendered
speechless by the smell
of obscene emasculation
but this morning
the sun wakes up
laughing with the sharp-edge
birth of retrieved root
nimble as dream
translated memory rides
past and future alike

RANDOM NOTES TO MY SON

Beware, my son, words
that carry the loudnesses
of blind desire also carry
the slime of illusion
dripping like pus from the slave's battered back
e.g. they speak of black power whose eyes
will not threaten the quick whitening of their own intent
what days will you inherit?
what shadows inhabit your silences?

I have aspired to expression, all these years,
elegant past the most eloquent word. But here now
our tongue dries into maggots as we continue our slimy
death and grin. Except today it is fashionable to scream
of pride and beauty as though it were not known that
'slaves and dead people have no beauty'

Confusion
in me and around me
confusion. This pain was
not from the past. This pain was
not because we had failed
to understand:
this land is mine
confusion and borrowed fears
it was. We stood like shrubs
shrivelled on this piece of earth
the ground parched and cracked
through the cracks my cry:

And what shapes
in assent and ascent
must people the eye of newborn
determined desire know
no frightened tear ever rolls on
to the elegance of fire. I have
fallen with all the names I am
but the newborn eye, old as
childbirth, must touch the day
that, speaking my language, will
say, today we move, we move ...

TO MOTHER

Toward the laughter we no longer know
this way we must from now on
and always, past shapes
turned into shadows of wish
and want, regret too. Your eye,
I know, is stronger than faith in
some god who never spoke our language

And here it seems to have been aborted.
Words, and they are old and impotent.
Here a slave will know no dance of laughter.

What of the act my eye demands
past any pretentious power of any word
I've known? My days have fallen
into nightmarish despair. I know
no days that move on toward laughter
except in memory stale as our glory
I see no touch of determined desire
past the impotence of militant rhetoric
the anguished twists of our crippled day will not
claim my voice. Woman dancer-of-steel
did you ever know that the articulate silence
of your eye possessed my breath for long days?
yet still I know no dance but the slow
death of a dazed continent

We claim the soil of our home
runs in our blood yet we run
around the world the shit of others
drooling over our eye. We know
no dance in our blood now but doom
so who are the newlyborn
who, unquestionable,
can claim the hands of the son?

TO MY DAUGHTER

There was a time
when I too thought eye
it was would take me
to the thrust of our intended
purpose. I did not know
this illusion, responding,
as I did, to word
with word.
                    Did we think this
was the way to family, to
protection? But the peasant can
still not stay until moonlight in the paddy
or mealiefield. Should you one day
see a man's back wobble to your eye
like a scab or pus over all
the wounds you have known
tell your sister or brother
your father was once a dreamer

TIME

This moment
        like a tyrant strides
        across sunrise and sunset
        claiming its own
        panoramic view
        no matter what the recorded lies

This moment
        like a tyrant strides
        across Soweto or
        Harlem streets painting
        tomorrows against today's
        fading moments of public hide and weep

And walks these
sidewalks with Ray Charles
Georgia on the mind
Is it not the right time!

INNUENDO

I heard voices
and anguished songs
in those days
I said listen
to the voices listen
to the cries of death
you laughed
at the pulse of my mind
in those days
we took time
to look at deeds
indeed we also saw
vipers' eyes rasping through
the hole where your life used to be
in those days
when you laughed
we took time to remember

LIKE THE TIDE: CLOUDWARD

    Turning here
  or returning there
a fractured rhythm from
the distant past makes demands

Or the image summoning
the existence of things
or exploding the core
of the sinister rot our minds must vomit
when the cloudward flood screams
and some panting and fear-ridden
wish to have been born without
as much as a teaspoonful of brain

              Soldiers or architects
we might have been. But here we stand torn
between academic masturbation and splitting
or chiselling words leaving the air unreddened
where for humanity a little wrench
would have sufficed for salvation. But
words, be they elegant
as verse or song
robust and piercing as sunshine
or hideous memories of our
cowardice in bondage are meaningless unless
they be the solid coil around our desire and method
or the 'most competent rememberer.' May we

    Turn here
  or return there
where a fractured rhythm from
the distant past moves us

TOWARDS A WALK IN THE SUN

The wind is caressing
the eve of a new dawn
a dream: the birth of
    memory

      Who are we? Who
were we? Things cannot go on much as
before. All night long we shall laugh
behind Time's new masks. When the moment
hatches in Time's womb we shall not complain

        Where oh where are the men
        to matches the fuse to burn
        the snow that freezes some
        wouldbe skyward desire

You who swallowed your balls for a piece
of gold beautiful from afar but far from
beautiful because it is coloured with the pus
from your brother's callouses. You who creep
lower than the snake's belly because you swallowed
your conscience and sold your sister to soulless
vipers. You who bleached the womb of your daughter's
mind to bear pale-brained freaks. You who bleached
your son's genitals to slobber in the slime of missionary-
eyed faggotry. You who hide behind the shadow of your master's
institutionalised hypocrisy the knees of your soul numbed
by endless kneeling to catch the crumbs from your master's table
before you run to poison your own mother. You too
deballed grin   you who forever tell your masters
I have a glorious past I have rhythm I have this
I have that. Don't you know I know all your lies?
The only past I know is hunger unsatisfied
and a kick in the empty belly
from your fat-bellied master
        And rhythm don't fill an empty stomach

Who are we? All night long
I listen to the dream soaring
like the tide. I yearn
to slit throats and colour
the wave with the blood of the villain
to make a sacrifice to the gods. Yea,
there is pain in the coil around things

Where are we? The memory ...
and all these years all these lies!
you too over there misplaced nightmare
forever foaming at the mouth forever
proclaiming your anger ... a mere
formality because your sight is coloured
with snow. What does my hunger
have to do with a gawdamm poem?

This wind you hear is the birth of memory
when the moment hatches in time's womb
there will be no art talk. the only poem
you will hear will be the spearpoint pivoted
in the punctured marrow of the villain; the
timeless native son dancing like crazy to
the retrieved rhythms of desire
fading
in-
to
memory

THE GODS WROTE

We are breath of drop of rain
Grain of sea sand in the wind
We are root of baobab
Flesh of this soil
Blood of Congo brush elegant
As breast of dark cloud
Or milk flowing through the groaning years

We also know
Centuries with the taste
Of white shit down to the spine

The choice is ours
So is the life
The music of our laughter reborn
Tyityimba or boogaloo passion
Of the sun-eyed gods of our blood
Laughs in the nighttime, in the daytime too
And across America vicious cities
Clatter to the ground. Was it not
All written by the gods!
Turn the things! I said
Let them things roll
To the rhythm of our movement
Don't you know this is a love supreme!

John Coltrane   John Coltrane tell the ancestors
We listened we heard your message
Tell them you gave us tracks to move
Trane and now we know
The choice is ours
So is the mind and the matches too
The choice is ours
So is the beginning
'We were not made eternally to weep'
The choice is ours
So is the need and the want too
The choice is ours
So is the vision of the day

RE/CREATION

The face in my head
was born to tears, moaning
in silence to the grin acknowledging defeat
to butchered smiles
and the anguish of a mother's tense womb

The face in my head
grows to the shape of a song
remembering yesterdays without laughter
remembering more than I will ever
know between lips or time

What you hear between
the silences
you are witness to
the lover's heart humming
the death of every thing
but acts of love
the steady hand at the trigger
moved by the heart whose
blood has been a witness to love
knowing that words
without the specific act
will hang frozen around
your face to condemn you before
any breath or breadth of life
or love

      To move towards
laughter has always been my desire
so here now knowing what
you should do you must do
right now I laugh
moved by the memory
of hate and guns and love

moved by my son's memory
whose face is yet to be born
in the name of the act
triggered by us when we know
armed peace is an act of love
rhythm
      is
         this,
            and clarity. The face
in my head remembering
more than I will ever know
and the eye out there before
the hand feeling the thens and
whys of yesterdays without laughter
knowing the fire of today's how
clasps the gun
that will set me free

MY NAME IS AFRIKA

for Nqabeni Mthimkhulu

All things come to pass
When they do, if they do
All things come to their end
When they do, as they do
So will the day of the stench of oppression
Leaving nothing but the lingering
Taste of particles of hatred
Woven around the tropical sun
While in the belly of the night
Drums roll and peal a monumental song
To every birth its blood
All things come to pass
When they do
We are the gods of our day and us
Panthers with claws of fire
And songs of love for the newly born
There will be ruins in Zimbabwe for real
Didn't Rap say,
They used to call it Detroit
And now they call it Destroyed!
To every birth its pain
All else is death or life

POINT OF DEPARTURE: FIRE DANCE FIRE SONG

A wise old man told me in Alabama: *Yeah, Ah believes in nonviolence awright.*
But de only way to stay nonviolen in dis man's country is to keep a gun an use it.
Four years earlier another wise old man had told me the same thing near
Pietersburg in South Africa. He said his words of wisdom in Sepedi.

1. THE ELEGANCE OF MEMORY

Distances separate bodies not people. Ask
Those who have known sadness or joy
The bone of feeling is pried open
By a song, the elegance
Of colour, a familiar smell, this
Flower or the approach of an evening …

All this is *now*

I used to wonder
Was her grave warm enough
Mmadikeledi, my grandmother
As big-spirited as she was big-legged
She would talk to me, she would
How could I know her sadness then
Or who broke my father's back?
But now …

The elegance of memory
Deeper than the grave
Where she went before I could
Know her sadness is larger
Than the distance between
My country and I. Things more solid
Than the rocks with which those sinister
Thieves tried to break our back

I hear her now. And I wonder
Now does she know the strength of the fabric
She wove in my heart for us? ... Her
Voice clearer now than then: Boykie
Don't ever take any nonsense from *them*
You hear!

        There are memories between us
Deeper than grief. There are feelings
Between us much stronger than the cold
Enemy machine that breaks the back
Sister, there are places between us
Deeper than the ocean, no distances
Pry your heart open, brother, mine too
Learn to love the clear voice
The music in the memory pried
Open to the bone of feeling, no distances

2. LUMUMBA SECTION

Searching past what we see and hear
Seering past the pretensions of knowledge
We move to the meeting place
The pulse of the beginning the end
And the beginning
In the stillnesses of the night
We see the gaping wounds where
Those murderers butchered your flesh
As they butchered the flesh of our land
Spirit to spirit we hear you
Then blood on blood comes the pledge
Swift as image in spirit and blood
The sons and daughters of our beginnings
Boldly move to post-white fearlessness
Their sharpnesses at the murderer's throat
Carving your song on the face of the earth
In the stillnesses of the night
Informed by the rhythm of your spirit
We hear the song of warriors
And rejoice to find fire in our hands
'Ain't no mountain high enough …' Dig it
The silences of the wind know it too
'Ain't no valley low enough …'
Freedom, how do you do!

3. FIRE DANCE

There will be no dreaming about escape
There will be no bullshit coldwar talk
The fire burns to recreate
the rhythms of our timeless acts
this fire burns timeless in our
time to destroy all nigger chains
as real men and women emerge
from the ruins of the rape by white greed

The rape by savages who want to control
us, memory, nature. Savages who even forge
measures to try to control time. Don't you know
Time is not a succession of hours
Time is always *now*, don't you know!
Listen to the drums. That there is a point of departure
Now is always the time. Praise be to Charlie Parker
And it don't have nothing to do with hours

Now sing a song of *now*
A song of the union of pastandfuture
Sing a song of blood – the African miner, his body
Clattering to the ground with mine phthisis
That there is murder. Do the dance of fire
The rhythm of young black men
Burning these evil white maniacs

Their greedy hands clattering to the ground
Like all their vile creations
Do our thing for the world, our world
Now's the time, *now*'s the time
A breath of love, song for my woman
Fire in her breast for our children
Supreme as a climax with the music
Of the wind. In her divine thigh
There is life there is fire

4. SPIRITS UNCHAINED

for Max Stanford

Rhythm it is we
walk to against the evil
of monsters that try to kill the spirit
It is the power of this song
that colours our every act
as we move from the oppressor-made gutter
Gut it is will move us from the gutter
It is the rhythm of guts
blood black, granite hard
and flowing like the river or the mountains
It is the rhythm of unchained spirit
will put fire in our hands
to blaze our way
to clarity to power
to the rebirth of real men

FOR IPELENG

to Gerry T & the students who unleashed it at Bennett

I saw her come here with no words
arms flailing air, past mother, thigh,
and blood. Here we begin again

We shall know each other
by the root of our appetite
or rhythm, Big Mama Juicy
Aneb seemed to say
Her eye direct as comment. As
roaches or rats. As heads cracked
open for fun or lawandorder
in this strange place

When I woke up one morning
I saw her coming in the stillness
of her day and want. My eye sprung out
to embrace a season of dreams
but she asked: if mother or father
is more than parent, is this my land
or merely soil to cover my bones?

THE PRESENT IS A DANGEROUS PLACE TO LIVE

1. IN THE MOURNING

And at the door of the eye
is the still voice of the land
My father before my father
knew the uses of fire
my father before my father
with his multiple godhead
sat on his circular stool
after the day was done. At times even
between the rednesses of two suns
knowing that time was not born yesterday

The circle continues
time will always be
in spite of minutes that know no life
Lives change in life
at times even rot
or be trampled underfoot
as the back of a slave
There are cycles in the circle
I may even moan my deadness
or mourn your death
in this sterile moment asking:

Where is the life we came to live?
Time will always be
Pastpresentfuture is always now
Where then is the life we came to live?

2. BEWARE OF DREAMS

The present is a dangerous place
to live. There were dreams once
riding past and future alike. We
embraced the dream, drunk past
any look at the present in the face

There were dreams once
and the illusion led
to the present

There were dreams once
gold, or red,/green&black
but the present is here
like me and you. And is articulate
And knows no peace. Neither do you
nor me if we are friends
enough to have known the dream

3. WITHOUT SHADOW

I live here now
among my silences
without life, an artifact
with as much use as a fart

I live here now
silent. And the silence
does not have the peace
of understanding wrung from the past

I live here now
without a shadow, but not even
dead since the dead are a vector
on the cycle of all that lives

Beware of dreams
they will so readily send
your eye shattering against nightmare
any time as any place you are alone
You will moan your impotence or mourn
the quick rotting of the seed
that could have been your life,
silently. Now shuttered, you may run deep
enough into knowledge to understand this decay
but your bony fingers remain so weak
they cannot seize even a moment

4. MIRRORS, WITHOUT SONG

Do not tell me, my brother, to reach out
and touch my soul. My soul
is inside and
thin
and knows your death too

Does it matter then how
often my teeth are seen
when I laugh less and less?

Morning does not wake up
with my eye out the window
moaning, or mourning,
a thing or day gone to waste

I die in the world
and live my deadness
in my head, laughing
less and less
Do you see now
another day, like a slave,
shows its face to be nothing
nothing but a mirror of the death of another?

When I laugh, my brother, less and less
do not tell me to reach
out and touch my soul. My soul
is inside and thin
and knows your death too

THERE ARE NO SANCTUARIES
EXCEPT IN PURPOSEFUL ACTION

1. WOUNDED WORD, INSANE SONG

At the sound of the insane who think themselves sane, death's certain laughter eats away the vein of a whole generation, leaving a legacy of spiritual and mental bankruptcy, and decay, for the next. Violence, then, documented past any argument by thousands of instant deaths in terror-stricken township nights, is turned inward. In piercing daylight too if you die you die. We were so cool, we thought, shrouded in some shit straight out of the pages of some american magazine.

We die,
> our unthinking lives aborted by the heedless
> blade or bullet of a crazed thug. Or by
> a hasty police baton, boot or bullet

We die,
> quaffing shakespeare, the magna carta, the queen's
> language and sipping four o'clock tea

We die,
> though we remain animate in the silences that gaze
> at us through the cracks which scar millions
> of hollow and twisted township hearts

The fifties,
the thick of all those whitenesses in our eye
which seems to refuse to learn anything about power

The fifties,
we are so bleached at our supposed hippest
we call america home, edladleni

The fifties,
but really any white time as any place
where our home is not our home

The fifties,
we live in a madhouse

The fifties,
this death is not new

And days that pass me by will pass
with legs heavier than the slave's
load. Presences shatter my sleep
with the strange brutality of the sun
on the back of a slave. Unable to move
I shout:

Getoutofhere you hideous mothafucka!

Because tomorrow should be a new day
Because tomorrow I should be older
I wonder if tomorrow I will be wiser

2. WHEN THINGS FALL APART

after & for Chinua Achebe

I lost my virginity and ran
into a world liced with whores

In the silences of the night
often past the midnight hour
when my voice dries up behind my tongue
behind corpses that rattle in my mind
I wonder where the wind is

If you are afraid of your reflection
do not come my way
at times I am a mirror

If I am a receptacle
you will see your life
and the particles of your death
collected in me

There is no serenity here
past the slow rattle of our quick decay
lying in ambush around the street corners

Mirror or receptacle where no dreams
come to roost in the night, I travel
from where we have been to where we might have been
through the silences, my prayer:

Sound, where did even beer cans
find your relationship to the wind!
Spirit, I could dub you tree as baobab
but where did your soil go?

3. EXILE

And the ocean, my brother knows, is not our friend
I wonder if our ancestors might also be
in exile in places I dare not call by name

Where I sit among my silences
where we yearn for a mood more ancient
than oceans, there is no community alarm

We try to begin again
but our dance is more waste
than the menstrual flow of a barren harem waif

'We are things of dry hours and the involuntary plan,
Grayed in, and gray.' We bleed. We bleed.
Everywhere we walk are the white footprints
Our skeletons rattle under them

Did you say independence?
There are words here, we know, as any
place. Desire. And other appetites with the sharp
brutality of a blunt knife against a gumful of pus

When even our temper is sucked
for fun and profit like a tit in a brothel
I know we are pawns in a pimp culture

Lumumba, do you hear us?
I stand among my silences
in search of a song to lean on
but our breath lacks the rapid rhythm of the river

Is community more forgotten now than last
week's handshake?
But the young are here.
They have ears.
They will try to sing.
What songs will move them from our deadness

4. PERCEPTION

for Gerry T and Roger D

Fire from stone on stone
to sound or magic
when night comes softly
the spirit is in ascent
her witness is music
warm touch early evening

Here is your ritual robe
here the grave of your dreams
stony cold and rusty
over there is the land of the rainbow
and other cities with their strange appetites

We search for the lost prayer
singing our magic song
to assemble the shattered pieces

5. LOGISTICS

i saw her try to rise to sun
against pillars of ice slippery as pus
i saw her try to rise to song

womanchild, fragrance of rose and divine rage rooted in
spirit fertile as my land now butchered by the devil's appetite
they whose eye is glued to the devil's rectum, how can they
know there is more open between us than your thighs

night, like the colour of our
desire, come bind us

but there are no distances here

even in the silence of the hotel room
whose fiction is too vicious for our dreams
night binds us like an oath

even against the hate and the hurt
of the vampire's teeth deep to our marrow
i taste the bone of our purpose
in the salt of your nipple

since the real man comes from his heart
i rise to offer you mine
where night binds us like an oath

NOTES FROM NO SANCTUARY

1.
There are no sanctuaries
except in purposeful action,
I could say to my child,
there are wounds deeper
than flesh. Deeper and more
concrete than belief is some god
who would imprison your eye
in the sterile sky instead of
thrusting it on the piece of earth
you walk every day and say,
Reclaim it

                                            But I let it pass
since it is really about knowing today and how
this is what it has come to. Daughters
and sons are born now and could ask,
you know: Knowing your impotence why
did you bring me here?

                                I could say
Life is the unarguable referent
what you know is merely a point
of departure. So let's move. But we have
been dead so long and continue. There will
be no songs this year. We no longer
sing. Except perhaps some hideous
gibberish like James Brown making believe
he is american or beautiful or proud. Or
some fool's reference to allah who, like
jehovah, never gave a two-bit shit about niggers

I could say, like Masekela,
We are in jail here. Which is
to say, we have done nothing
I could say ... but see,
what difference does it make
as long as we eat white shit?
no matter what it is wrapped up in

2.
How many deaths and specific
how or when ago was it
the rememberer said, where
to go is what to do?

        Still we talk somuch!

And cold black hustlers of my generation claw
their way into the whitenesses of their desire
and purpose. Here a slave's groan and shudder
is a commodity the hustler peddles newly-wrapped
in brother, sister, revolution, power to the people ...

        So now having spoken our time or referent,
        a people's soul gangrened to impotence,
        all the obscene black&whitetogether kosher
        shit of mystified apes ... Where then is
        the authentic song? The determined
        upagainstthewallmothafucka act?

        So say you say you float above
        this menace, having violently tasted
        white shit past the depths of any
        word you know. Say you float above
        the dollar-green eye of the hustler whose
        purpose is cloaked in dashikis and glib
        statements about revolution

        Say you float

untouchably above this menace, does
your purpose, if there be one, propose
to be less impotent than this poem?

THE SAME STRIP OF LAND

Wouldbe brother hear me well
this voice I bring you
is the voice of our mothers
fathers of my father and your peers
you … you are your own father

Listen carefully
the ancients say
the finger of the witch
points at you and withdraws to the witch
but the word that is uttered
does not return to the tongue
any more than a deed could be undone

The bridge or strip of land
that allows you to go
across it to give reports
to those who massacre even infants
is the same
that keeps some away from home
for years too many to remember
that keeps some away so long
they do not have any memories of home
though at night they see the lights
where they dream and fight to return

Hear me well
the voice I bring you
is not from Moscow
remember bridge or strip of land
gets people together or keeps them apart

Listen carefully
when the womb of our mothers
hears your name mentioned
the womb sings a sad song

RITES OF PASSAGE

The road signs welcoming the traveller
to Lusaka used to warn us
do not get there dead
just get there

We do get weary yes
and die for warmth and tenderness
and so do our children

Do not think the child
does not have nightmares
similar to yours

When we get weary
die for warmth and tenderness
and die in the heat of our time
wonder if the ice we do not even have
memory of is not stretching its hideous hand
to shake our weary one
do not think it is beyond the clear grasp
of the child's anguish
turned to want and need

Wouldbe poet stop boring us
with how sensitive you are
show us what it is
to be man woman child
in want of warmth and tenderness

DANCE

Siamese twin
Of song
We said a while back
We are music people

In the spell of Tombouctou
We ransack the origin of experience
Stride through the corridors of history and myth
And bounce back to here and now

Madiba Salute Comrade
Thank you for introducing us
To Sankore to Bouctou
Ancient legend vibrant Mali
Meeting point of fact and myth
Amidst harmattan of flower and sand
Where humanity survives and survives

MORNING IN TUNIS

for Zweli and Katlego

Of the paradise and glory
Of the never-ever time
Of a place none can point at
No matter how many preachers are born
There will be no celebration of life
Except where memory collected and collective
From then now and then guides us

Now even though
My children have never known peace
I would like the children of the world
To see with their ear
And sing the sunrise in Tunis

It is heart-of-watermelon red
Mellow like an amber slice of moon
As it emerges from high rock and low cloud
Suspended near the bluesless sky
A spectre between nothing and nothing
Without a single ray of light
As if simply to say
Don't you know the world is remarkable

LUTHULI DETACHMENT

In the depths of night
my heart is an incendiary
but the flames do not offer any light

Prayer yields no result in life
program will   and does
as the young say
Tambo give me the machine
that will deliver my day

We must redden
the blackest folds
of our memory and intent

Some say in delirium
that the Luthuli Detachment is ancient detail
without relevance or meaning now
as if an antique walks among us

You traitor who has defiled
your mother's womb
with your tongue glued
to the stench
in your master's voluminous bowels
you whose conscience
is lower than that of the worm
may maggots and red ants gnaw
at where your lifeline might have been
until the earth stops rotating

Chris Slovo what is conspiracy
if the enemy knows who was between
whose thighs last night
and has so many children as evidence
what hideous ambush will force us
to name the enemy among our ranks

Questions loom when the lights are dark
in broad daylight too   pushing us
against the walls of our silence
if our tongue remains tight on the palate
who are we going to sing as hero of heroes

Oh future memory unbind these tangles
hear now Duma feverish like a dream
with his pioneer eye fixed beyond this menace
pierces these frustrated walls with the warrior dance
heita … heita … kuth'angihlanye … ngihlanye!

Poet do not sedately scratch
the outer trimmings of your voice
when here and now a monster heaves and rustles
among the flames of an incendiary
more hideous than the end of peace

WHEN THE CLOUDS CLEAR

She takes no part
in the prime of my slow death
after so many years
she remains foreign
to any form of suicide

Tonight there is no smile
from the remote corners of her eye
lightning flashes and thunder
blast me to smithereens
from the corners of her eye

She takes no part
in the prime of my slow death

Her nerves are stretched irrational now
but stupidity much older than my generation
or I will ever be
pushes me into flames where
there is no elegance of eloquence

Oh my mothers and fathers of my father
you who are wiser than I will ever be
please please tell me
why it is that my foolishness
must hurt these loved ones
when the deadly mortars of enemy fire
are here with us
every day and night

If you see my back
wobbling down these mean streets
without memory or desire
without fire of hope or conviction
know I killed the fragrance
of her hope and desire

What had the ancients observed
when they said of cattle
when I lack it
I have no sleep
when I have it
I still lack sleep
remember only yesterday someone said
something makes you do right
the same thing makes you do wrong
singing about love and happiness

So when we tame this turbulence
it will not be without pain
it will not be without pain
if memory can be witness
and could claim some wisdom
mother used to say
in the crucible of life
it is what you value most
that will cause the most pain

So when we tame this turbulence
it will not be without pain
it will not be without pain

Or should I just plead
like the blues singer
hit me in the eye
maybe then maybe then
I'll see better
because when I search the crevices of my voice
I do not want to say anything unreal
as the ancients say
when the clouds clear
we shall know the colour of the sky

RED SONG

Need I remind
      Anyone again that
Armed struggle
      Is an act of love

I might break into song
Like the bluesman or troubadour
And from long distance
In no blues club
I might say
      Baby baby baby
There is no point in crying
Just because just because I'm not at home

When I try to run away from song
Walking softly in the night
A persistent voice
More powerful than the enemy bombs
Grabs me by the elbow of my heart
Demanding the song
That bathes our lives
In the rain of our blood
Stretched taut in the streets
As Moloise gasps the last breath
Of one solitary life

Should I now stop singing of love
Now that 'my memory is surrounded by blood'
Sister why oh why
Do we at times mistake
A pimple for a cancer
And you brother
Who knows our tough tale
Who has been through the tunnel
On this long road
Who has seen the night winking and whispering

Who possesses the worldwide hands
Of the worker
Who has created
This house these clothes this bed
This street I walk in the night
This light to shatter the darkness of this despair
Tell me why
I must not sing a song of love

Horror and terror are not strangers
When Duma no older than six years
Looks at shoeprints in the yard
And says: Papa who has been here
Rrangwane Uncle Thami Uncle Tim Uncle George
And you do not have shoes like this
Mama why did you leave
The window open
The child knows and tells
Something about the life
We live

So who are they who say
No more love poems

I want to sing a song of love
For the woman who blasted the boers
Out of that yard across the border
And lived long enough to tell it
I want to sing a song of love
For that woman who jumped fences
And gave birth to a healthy child
I want to sing a song of love
For that old woman who in fearful nights
Still gave refuge to comrades
I want to sing a song of love
For the peasant who shared
His meagre supper with comrades
Without 'returns for services rendered'

So now with my hands
Clasping guns grenades bombs
Embracing the warmth of my woman's breast
Moving to the rhythm of a mother's love
And the sadsad eye of a father
Embraced in the fixed demands
Of a troubled and expectant people
From the stench of history
And the fragrance of desire and purpose
Softly I walk into the embrace
Of this fire that will ignite
My song of love
My song of life

FOR OLINKA

To wander, the ancients say,
is to see. And, in seeing,
perhaps wonder about the road
that shapes who we are
or destroys
who we might have been

There then is where
the childhood of our memory
collected like grain in the harvest season
or nipped in the bud like seed in the drought

Olinka
the path of the vision
of my mothers and kinsmen
has made you
my pride and joy
not that stubborn questions
never invade our restless moments
that is the dangerous luxury
only the dead of heart and head enjoy

Whether you and I
or anyone else or creature
who walk this earth
 believe in any superstition
native or imported and imposed
through bible colonial twin of rifle
is not any of our doubt or fear now

On the day I became your father
a cord powerful as Life's twins
Birth and Death bound us like an oath
in a house some believe
belongs to some god even
children have not seen build anything
ask anyone whose home
is desire and nightmare
because to be alive
you must have somewhere to go

The sun that rises in the east
and sets in the west
anywhere on this planet
also knows
we want somewhere to go
to laugh to love to play
to work to enjoy the life
we came to live

SEAPARANKOE

The need of the land we sing, the flowers
Of manhood, of labour, of spring;
We sing the deaths that we welcome as ours
And the birth from the dust that is green we sing
COSMO PIETERSE

Malome your body has followed Duma's
In less than the nine months
That follow the blood of the moon
Bidding the mother to usher humanity here

Your body is down under now
Down under Seaparankoe
And predictably there are fools here
Who still cannot know that
The Kotanekind can neither fall nor fail

Our hearts and heads
Remain pliable in the easy embrace
Of your worldwide hands
For generations they will remain
Pliable like dough
Turning to bread
In the worker's hands
Or words turning
To embers of wisdom and courage
At the bidding of the poet's heart

But Seaparankoe the mouths of fools
Who do not know
That no power on this planet
Could ever kill all humanity
Or stay our desire for liberty and peace
Are here with us
From the perverse core of their greed

Every person must work or fight
That is the simple truth we learn
From your life and love
Which rules and enhances our vision
Out of the lethal stench of the intemperate present

Here I do not bury or freeze my tears
Salty as the sea accomplice
In the crime and rancid slime
Of pogroms class clashes genocide
Across the taut belly of this planet

Under your vision which commands
Our conscience and consciousness
With easy affection as my brother tells
I say yes to the tears and the sea
I say yes and fashion them
Into the instrument and fruit
Of our informed and determined
Want and purpose
I say yes Malome
We must be bolshevised
I say yes
Every person must work or fight
I say yes
Kotane is dead
But Kotanekind can neither fall nor fail

Come Malome come
Come we say
Not that we are dotard enough
To think we can bring back the dead
Kotanekind come bind us
Come bind the poets
Come make of our music
The sound of the gun
That will set us free
To create   to laugh   to work
And sing the deaths that we welcome as ours
And the birth from the dust that is green
Not that we are strangers to fear
But we love freedom and peace more
And for this we work and fight

A LUTA CONTINUA

Requiem for Duma Nokwe

If in ritual delirium we felt
your death had isolated us
we would join the song:
Sunshine, blue sky, please go away
but Duma son of our crisis
how could we cry at your death
if the peace and brotherhood you lived for
continues to live in us! Amandla!

Your name informed by our bloodstains
was born before your body
to inform us:
A workers' world is ascending
over the stench and sunken graves
of these racists rapists goldfanged exploiters

Duma, child of my mother
your body has left us yes
that is a boundary
we had not expected so soon
you taught us, though, that boundaries
and oceans merely separate bodies not people

There are men, Che said,
who find their hereafter
among the people
life and victory as you knew
and lived it in all the *names*
that in dying for life
make life surer than death
will continue to spring and flower
from mother's womb and earth's bowels
from hand of warrior and worker too

If the warped bloodhounds of tyranny say
they will torture and kill us
let them. Let them
skulls they will crack yes
young bones they will trample underfoot
yes. School and church will also try
to twist and break our young yearning minds yes

But the unbridled brutality of these beasts
shall not break us. We are not twigs
your love for humanity and peace
strengthens us. We now clearly know
a worker's world is ascending

Duma child of my mother
there are men who find their hereafter
among the people
you live forever in us
you are all the names
that in dying for life
make life surer than death

Poet leave him alone you have praised him
if you sing of workers you have praised him
if you sing of liberation you have praised him
if you sing of brotherhood you have praised him
if you sing of peace you have praised him
you have praised him without knowing his name
his name is Spear-of-the-Nation. Mayibuye!

NEW AGE

The questions which have always been here
jump at us like impatient lovers
of nights which cannot be numbed
not even by spirits departed from bottle or land

when fogs of despair jump up thick in our heads
when struggle becomes the next bottle
or the warmth between a willing woman's thighs
sucking into her our hasty greed
remember O comrade commander of the ready smile
this is pain and decay of purpose

Remember in baton boot and bullet ritual
the bloodhounds of Monster Vorster wrote
SOWETO over the belly of my land
with the indelible blood of infants
so the young are no longer young
not that they demand a hasty death

The past is also turbulent
ask any traveller with memory
to tame it today is our mission
with liberty hammered to steel in our eye

Remember O Poet
when some of your colleagues meet
they do not talk the glories of the past
or turn their tongues blackwards
in platitudes or idealistic delirium
about change through chance or beauty
or the perversion you call love
which be nothing   nothing
but the mercenary pairing of parasites

The young whose eyes carry neither youth nor cowardice
the workers whose song of peace
now digs graves for these goldfanged fascist monsters
with artistic precision and purpose
now know the past is turbulent
we must tame it now
ask any eye fuelled with liberty

Tell those with ears to hear   tell them
tell them my people are a garden
rising out of the rancid rituals of rape and ruin
Tell them   tell them in the dry season
leaves will dry and fall to fertilise the land
whose new flowers black green and gold
are a worker's song of fidelity
to the land that mothered you

SOUTH AFRICA SALUTES UZBEKISTAN

We shall dream yes
and when history absolves us
we shall be celebrants

In sunbathed Uzbekistan
land of reclaimed desert
the Hungry Steppe now feeds
and clothes land and patriot
and any visitor in solidarity
under 250 days of uninterrupted sunshine

Here we are celebrants
sucking the succulent
ladies' fingers

Tashkent, Samarkand, Soviet Asia
monument of the past
and beacon of tomorrow
Salute! In the name
of my people with my hand
upon my heart which I offer you
from South Africa and the ANC
good day young pioneers with all
those flowers and faces for the peace
your peers have never known in my country

Here we are celebrants of our future
here we witness the step towards the wholeness
we seek. Here we say *Yes*!
like the erstwhile Hungry Steppe
where desert under human hand
has given up its impartial brutality
for cotton for fruit for flower
for people's power

We are not the sole witness and celebrant here
Vietnam says Yes. Cuba and Chile … Si!
MPLA triumphant and determined beyond
what any puppet or imperialist monster
would like to see in this world is here
here in the land of Lenin
is PAIGC, PLO and those whose children
will condemn for having called themselves nonaligned
when the lines of our struggle and choice
are drawn with mathematical precision

Here we have not seen beggars
we have not seen children
with ribs like guitar strings
to condemn the fat-bellied swine
who slobber on the dreams of freedom lovers
we have not seen mothers forced
to send their offspring to any stinking street
to peddle human juice for meal or drink
here we have not seen the humiliation of tyranny
the fear the loathing of oneself
which my brother has known and told
here humanity will live and flourish

Yes Uncle J.B.
Yes Malome
Yes Dadoo
Sisulu, Fischer Yes
With clenched ANC fist
for people's power and my small hand
upon the banner for the peace we must fight for
Yes

Salute, Tovarishee, we are celebrants
of your present and our future
Amandla! Comrades. As Castro knows
History will absolve us
Yes to electrification
Yes to irrigation
Yes to industrialisation
Yes to desert reclaimed
Yes to solidarity
Yes to freedomsong
Yes Lenin, we shall dream
we shall turn that dream into reality
palpable as this cotton this flower
this fruit this love
Mayibuye!

WHAT TIME IS IT?

ANC's 77th anniversary

For seventy-seven years
rainclouds have been gathering
around my heart

        Come Thunder!

Come even on a clear day
come pierce the swollen womb
of these clouds. Let the rain
rage and rave
Come Thunder

        Come Hailstorm

If home is in the furnace of the womb of my eye
if home is where heart and head always are
I am the man on his way home
if peace is exile
if peace is moving north and north
we do not want peace

DUMALISILE

SOMAFCO 10th anniversary

Yes I am Solomon Mahlangu
Always the way forward yes
Death could never silence me
My blood will never be mute
Yes

I have outlived nights
and endless days of agony
I have outlived more terror
than the maddogs of this world can unleash

The song of my blood has caressed
the calloused and withered hands of the old woman
who in rags washes the robes of her torturers every day
the song of my blood is in the mines
in a plate of food
in that page a window into life
in the streets that erupt with violence or love
the song of my blood
is in the mind and passion of the youth
whose eye has been reddened with determined resolve

They tried to remove me from speech
they tried to exile me to silence
but my song elegant as the rainbow
thunders on a clear day
piercing the eardrum of their arrogance
like the spear of my ancestors
the same spear that the sons and daughters
of my song pierce the enemy
of their childhood games with
as they dance to the memory of days to come

Bana ba thari e ntsho
kana bangwe bo ba ka mpotsa
gore gatwe kgangkgolo ke eng
ba itira okare ga ba itse
gore nna ga ke utlwane le gobalabala
kana ga ke monna ke mosimane
ke tla siamelwa ke ditsame sentle fela
ka ke sa leke goipagololela megodu

I am the children of the future
I come dressed in the rainbow
of the flames of my song
didn't you hear my brother say
White people must learn to listen
Black people must learn to talk
Kalushi is talking now

Do not mourn me now
I am a celebrant here

Children of the nurturing skin *(abba-vel)* / some might dare to ask what the
farce is about / pretending not to know / that I do not suffer the emptiness of
chatter / take note I am in no hurry to be a man / my boyhood suits me just
fine / that way I get what is my due / without pre-empting anything

I AM

Beware my friend
I might be millions or more
things than what you have convinced
yourself I am
               I am
                    what I am

Without apology or hypocritical regret
when sound grabs me
and hurls me into the heat of music
I can be a Coltrane Coleman Dolphy solo out there
and deeper than any word you know
probing and exploring
every crevice and slice of life
from now to all pasts
presents and any plethora of futures
to bring you edibles

I can be tree
loving branches swinging
in the arms of wind
luxuriant leaves in their green laughter
with the sun

I could be an infant
teardrops at the eyelash
without a word
challenging you
to name the reason
behind the tears
since you say you know it all

I could be maddog willie
annoyed past any saying of it
by an idiotic question like
don't you think there is a danger
that the ANC might be misguided
by the Communists

Then I could be the ghoul
in your nightmare
which hurls you out of bed
and sleep wet with cold sweat
because you have just heard
that communists and terrorist monsters
have taken over the country and they say
the land belongs to those who work it

Of a night in Cape Town
I could be that angry young comrade
who insists through his liquor fumes
he democratically wants things a certain way
who insists clean your place first democratically
who does not democratically realise
his place is not too clean

I could be CAP
through the tongue of my walls
saying it is time we took art
out of the galleries
and on to the streets

I could be that crazy
little South African poet who insists
that the heights or flights of
                artistic exploration
or the depths that any
                artistic expression
might plunge into must
be dialectically related to
                social relevance

I could be Nadine
insisting that the writer
must seriously handle language
through the texture of life

I could be millions of what
I am
     just as
         I am
             just as
                  I am

MONTAGE: BOUCTOU LIVES

Even nature at her best
in singing her mesmerising beauty
with the permanent rainbow
that is the wonder of Mosioathunya
says nothing of the woman of Mali

My Mali sisters are a rainbow
even the deaf and dumb
would aspire to sing

Here Keats would have found voice
and song instead of the finality
of deadness
he dubs beauty and love
though we do not see human gesture
nor life in his Grecian urn

My sisters of Mali could
    teach any rainbow
        the impartial beauty
            of nature through a rainbow
of centuries of memory and mutations

Look at the flow of that ebony
elegance walking that walk
striding through your heart
turning Bamako into a dream
and that blue-eyed ivory contrast over there
that strut is a vector on the graph
linking Africa to where
and all of that all in
between bespeaks where

Which woman have you not met here
in Mali I have seen my mother
my daughter I have seen
my grandmother and her very own too
my wife   friends   comrades
all the women I love and hurt
all the women without whom
I am not even here
all the women without whom
neither you nor I
could claim an identity
which all that lives has

I wish I had enough
art of eloquence and grace to sing
the woman of Mali

HEART TO HEART

Without even thought to it
they suddenly clearly know
they could never have a love affair
such vulgarity would be an attempt to return
some place they have never been together

They are not in love
they never will be
they simply love

The rhythm of her legs
walking towards him is song
the call and response of life itself
is her eye engulfing all of him
and when her lips touch his
heart to heart
they drum to the same beat
oblivion takes over the whole world

And Fire from now on
from this moment on Fire
they are not consumed no
they are a streak of black lightning
through layers upon layers of song

Without even vaguest thought to it
they now clearly know
they could never have a love affair
perhaps now like Mayakovsky
he is not even a man
he is a cloud in pants

They are not in love
they never will be
they simply love

Poet t'under go drop I'm telling you
I did not say I could build castles
out of any single grain of sand
but I have spoken I
mouth that tells no lies
have spoken don't I say

Your eyes she says look out searching
but at the same time she says
your eyes search looking in

EVEN SKIN DISAPPEARS

Where he feels
      He might explode
           To smithereens

But here don't we know
There are no enemy explosives
Which reduce one to tiny
Strips of biltong scorched
And clinging to walls and trees

Where no part of the body
Is recognisable from any other
Here boundaries between two people
Disappear. Even skin
As everything else disappears
Even thought takes leave of absence

There are no separate identities here
The sword in the ceiling of her thigh disappears
Language itself rendered speechless disappears
Where would any naming of this new arrangement come from

REQUIEM FOR MY MOTHER

As for me
The roads to you
Lead from any place
Woman dancer-of-steel
Mother daughter sister
Of my young years
The roads to you
Lead from any place
I am

              I do not know
If you hollered in delirium
Like an incoherent dotard
I do not know if you gasped
For the next breath
Gagging
Fighting to hold your life
In.

              I do not know
If you took your last breath
With slow resignation
But this I know

I dare not look myself
In the eye peeled red
With despair and impotent regret
I dare not look myself
In the ear groaning
Under these years and tears
I dare not mourn your death
Until I can say without
The art of eloquence
Today we move we move

As for me
I will never again see
The slow sadness of your eye
Though it remains fixed
And talks through a grave
I do not know

I teeter through
The streets of our anguish
Through this incontinent time and referent
And when I try to scream *Vengeance*
My voice limps
Under the cacophony of them
Whose tongue is glued
To the bloodstains in the imperial
Monster's hallways and appetite

As for me
The roads to you
Lead from any place
Though I will never again
Know the morning odour
Of your anxious breath:
Don't let the sun shine
In your arse my child
We do not do those things
Though I will never again
Know your armpit odour
Before the ready-for-work mask
Though I will never again
See the slow sadness of your smile
Under the sun
Woman mother daughter sister
The slow sadness in your eye
Remains fixed and talks
Even here where the amber bandages
Of the sun kiss the day
Before they disappear beyond
These whitehooded mountains and appetites

FOR CECIL ABRAHAMS

With you I have refound the memory of my blood
And necklaces of laughter round my days
DAVID DIOP

Mirror of my pain and purpose
This blood we demand
Is the flow of life
We must bleed yes
There is no birth without blood
If they call us insane let them
Words will not kill us
If they say we are not poets let them
Our poetry will be the simple act
The blood we bleed
Moulded by pain and purpose
Into a simple
Do not fuck with me
Your shit is going up in flames
Here and now

FOR MONTSHIWA & PHETOE

it is time to make the time
I ⬥e with my skin and hear with my tongue
HENRY DUMAS

When you see me in misery
It is not tears I lack

Fire … out of my navel my song
Fire, come bind us. Fire, we aspire
To your elegance. Fire, come burn
These evil maniacs and their vile creations
Fire, it is your impartial evil
And your simple warmth
We aspire to

We do not aspire to blackness
That is locked in my navel
We do not aspire to compassion
That we have never lacked
We aspire to sons and daughters
Of postwhite fearlessness and outrage
We aspire to the story
Indelible on my brother's eye

When you see me in misery
It is not tears I lack

And when I reach into my navel
Into the soil that buries my mother
Turned shadow and companion to nightmare
And these eyes reaching for wind
To put fire in our hands
And when fire binds us
Fire of hate Fire of love
Fire out of slime of exile
Fire out of sense and need
Fire of want and demand
When fire binds us
Out of my navel my song

And when you see me in misery
It is not tears I lack

PLACES AND BLOODSTAINS

Notes for Ipeleng

> *It's none too soon*
> *to learn the signs:*
> *See that bird over there*
> *poised on a wingspan*
> *to ride the storm –*
> *the bird knows its enemies:*
> *that's the abc of it …*
>   EZEKIEL MPHAHLELE

You are what you do
beyond any saying of it

For the eye and the ear leaning and groaning
under the weighted centuries of rape and ruin
For the eye and the ear pried open by hunger
by the back peeled raw by the flame and the whip
of bible and rifle contact under any sky
For the eye and the ear wishing and wanting
to rid the slave years of their menace
I lean on the groaning years like the wind
searching their crevices for the life
we came to live

The world remains real
Man and appetite create or destroy
need and want twin parents of demand
where form is a willing servant
of memory and direction
where reason and decision
must destroy illusion
to mother energy and action
to nourish soul and purpose

After birth life must follow
and what you do reflects
nothing but your allegiance

Not that I have been to any mountaintop
where the sun wipes her nose before she shows
or hides her face. But this I know:
People are not mountains. They will meet
where and if they meet where the bloodstains are
the beginning of birth or burial. Not that the bones
that rattle under the sea
could not be your very own. Not that
what is eroded or trampled
underfoot and lost
could not become strange or alien
but that the juice that flows
oozes from the fruit or the sore
Not that language could ever be life
but that the hurt that tears laughter
from the eye and gives fire
to the word is more often a sign
of expectations betrayed than of hatred
Not that bloodstains are always a sign of death
Ask any mother who has known
sadness or joy

People are not mountains
they will meet where and if they will
not that there will be no bloodstains
and I repeat it here
while I can see:

> see that bird over there
> poised on a wingspan
> to ride the storm –
> the bird knows its enemies

In your young years
it is not strange or evil
to be childish. But stay away
from the stench of the childish old
After birth life must follow
and the roads that scar this earth
are impartial or treacherous therefore
I take my brother's voice and repeat:
it's never too soon to learn the signs

Even the ocean cannot claim innocence
the ocean is witness and accomplice
the waves stagger with scattered skeletons
and bloodstains. You cannot cry, though,
all tears taste like seawater

And you, like me
like any river or creature
like any season or drum
will move any and every day
to a particular rhythm
without even thought to it

We live under the sun,
if we do, and die here
when we do, where all is
collected, collective, and old
as childbirth or death

We wish and want
and have tragic memories
though our life is so hideously
prosaic. The bitterness of this
earth is pawn and parasite
and the elegant tongue is not
reliable like the simple act in
the snakepit we are in. Do not lose
your mind, though, or wear it like a wig
or damp drawers, like a cashmere cardigan
of a Sophiatown summerday
destined for instant death

We also know though
other songs and other places
like the rapid rhythm
when we slip and slide
into and through our jive
like: how could you lose
if you choose the stuff I use
or the slow elegance
when you walk that walk
and carry the meaning
in the rhythm and be
saying, without a word:
Don't it make you feel good!

Though you know that you
like Ananse, cannot claim
any virginity. Though you know
you do not have to be limp-minded
just because you have been violated
past any saying of it. Though you know
other places where the bloodstains
don't say anything about rape

After birth life must follow
but now when my voice limps away
from my tongue like a casualty
with bloodstains to testify
under any sky, searching
for the simple act, the re-
assembling of our shattered
and scattered pieces, what
it brings back, riding
the exhausted night
which is treacherous
as the sun, as the whip
or the Mississippi tree
where the bloodstains
chronicle this history, what
the voice brings back is a sadsad song

RECOLLECTIONS

Spring up and advance
Or retreat
Into and out of memory
You think you have finally
Started on a decisive journey
Away from the Africa of colonial design
Along with that of the narcissistic poets

You pause
Here
In search of direction
If your destination remains
Elusive
How do you propose
To know what direction to take

Though you remain
Convinced
To be alive
You must have somewhere
To go
Your destination remains
Elusive

Habits of movement rattle and peep
Through the silences
Surrounding your memory
As they ambush
What might have been
Clarity of in- or fore-sight
Or thought
But did you not only yesterday
Say where to go is what to do

Dizzy says:
It's taken all my life
To learn what not to play
How long will it take you
To learn what not to say?

VENCEREMOS

Says Consolata our lady
Of the soft vision
The gaze of the blind:
I will teach you
What you are hungry for

Thank you Toni

So questions jump up naked and agitated
Pushing us into the tightening vice
Of inconsolable memories
Demanding resolution

In love we are a quest
As in the rest of what
We are most responsive to
We must know though
The road to fulfilment
Is never s
t
r
a
i
g
h
t

I love you you are mine
Must never be allowed to mean
Anything about ownership or submission

I love you you are mine
Must mean fellow traveller
We are celebrants
Like the mother who knows
Sadness and joy
Like any birth it will not be
Without the tearing of tissue
Ask my sister who fears
The end of peace who knows
Where the kind kills are

We are like this poem
A quest and a sacrifice
So even when we bite lip in anguish
Even when a response or its absence
Threatens to mock our dream to abortion
When we find out as Ornette
Who is griot who is dreamkeeper
And the very way forward
When we find out we can
Make mistakes we will know
We are on to something
And this is why and how
The blues jumps clean out of pain
To immerse us in a vibrant celebration
Of life

Poet leave it   leave the heart alone
It has depths words will never reach
Leave it alone to wander as it will
To its heights of ecstasy
Or its depths of contemplation
Like the blues

AFFIRMATION

The sound of her voice
weaves a song with meaning
past the depths of any word
that might try to name
or bridle and tame it

In the sound of her voice
I remember every thing
I will never forget

Love might not be all
That a person needs
But it does count

Here with my little hand upon
The tapestry of memory and my loin
I once again lean on the blues to find voice:
If loving you is wrong
I don't want to do right

MEMORIAL

Though we know
Life is no long joy
Someone enters your life
And stays there

       You learn
Something about desire
And learn to live here
What is revealed is subtle
Though quiet it is equally intense
A flame not red but blue
Its contours vividly simplified and softer
Once here you seldom want to leave

When you stumble upon stillnesses
And such curious spaces without warning
You think you miss your old place
Where memories stayed within immediate reach

You now have difficulty finding memories
It is perhaps the lack of history
Yet peeking at you
Are images of beginnings
That have become soft remembrances
You turn over and over
Wondering at their comfort

IF I COULD SING

I want to remain
Wild
Like a young song
Unleashed
Aspiring
To the serenity
Of a Japanese morning
Hour
In which not a single leaf
Stirs above
Water stone and tree
If I could sing
Like Neruda I would
Weave a song about
The size of your worldwide heart

RENAISSANCE

I remount the curve of evil times
to unearth my anchored memory
ABDELLATIF LAABI

Again I say
I am music people
the cadence of what
we are moved by and move to
informs my eye
which does not want to risk
even a blink
for fear I might miss

some essential gesture
of the life we must live
in all its robustness
and sing as hours here
or any where we choose
breaking through all the silences
in the crevices of our turbulent memory

soundman
that I have always aspired to be
my ear sees the tentacles
of our fragile voice
breaking through the walls of our exiles
as I remount the curve of evil times
to unearth my anchored memory

REJOICE

Says Thebe Neruda of the vibrant smile
The eye so curious it is reluctant
To shut the world out even in sleep
I am the dreamkeeper he says
The spontaneous song and the dance
Pulsating with the force of my people's ethos
Watch me
    And rejoice

Our sister Betty Carter
Repository of our memory
Whose mouth is free of all untruth
Who plays her voice as a horn
Says you can do anything
You want to do
If you know what to do

I am witness and celebrant here
I do everything I want to do
Because I know what to do
I am the dreamkeeper I say
The mouth that tells no lie
I am not a man
I am a boy
Beneficiary of the fruit
Harvested from my people's memory
Watch me
    And rejoice

Poet leave him
Leave him alone
You have praised him
You have praised him
Without knowing his name
His name is Mouth-that-tells-no-lie

ACKNOWLEDGEMENTS

The poems have been selected from the following collections:

From SPIRITS UNCHAINED (Broadside Press, Detroit, 1969):
When brown is black; Brother Malcolm's echo; Mandela's sermon; To Fanon

From FOR MELBA (Third World Press, Chicago, 1970):
Origins; Song for Melba; Indeed in deed; Of death and lives; Death doses – 3; My people when nothing moves; Of us for us

From MY NAME IS AFRIKA (Doubleday, New York, 1971):
The air I hear; Shotgun; Mayibuye iAfrika; Random notes to my son; To mother; To my daughter; Time; Innuendo; Like the tide: Cloudward; Towards a walk in the sun; The gods wrote; Re/creation; My name is Afrika; Point of departure: Fire dance fire song: 1. The elegance of memory, 2. Lumumba section, 3. Dance, 4. Spirits unchained

From: THE PRESENT IS A DANGEROUS PLACE TO LIVE
(Third World Press, Chicago, 1975; 2nd ed. 1993):
For Ipeleng; The present is a dangerous place to live; 1. In the mourning, 2. Beware of dreams, 3. Without shadow, 4. Mirrors, without song; There are no sanctuaries except in purposeful action: 1. Wounded word, insane song, 2. When things fall apart, 3. Exile, 4. Perception, 5. Logistics; Notes from no sanctuary

From WHEN THE CLOUDS CLEAR (COSAW, Johannesburg, 1990):
The same strip of land; Rites of passage; Dance; Morning in Tunis; Luthuli detachment; When the clouds clear; Red song; For Olinka; Seaparankoe; A luta continua; New age; South Africa salutes Uzbekistan

From TO THE BITTER END (Third World Press, Chicago, 1995):
What time is it?; Dumalisile; I am; Montage: Bouctou lives; Heart to heart; Even skin disappears; Requiem for my mother; For Cecil Abrahams; For Montshiwa and Phetoe; Places and bloodstains

NEW WORK:
Recollections; Venceremos; Affirmation; Memorial; If I could sing; Renaissance; Rejoice